Reminders Life Is Good

Chantel Beckett

BookLeaf Publishing

Presentation by *BookLeaf Publishing*

Web: www.bookleafpub.com

E-mail: info@bookleafpub.com

ISBN: 9789357696777

First edition 2023

DEDICATION

For Tamara, my beautiful daughter, the light of my life, my reason to smile. You are my world, you bring me happiness. More than id thought possible watching your grow. I love you more than words can ever say.

For my Mum and Dad. After all we have been through, let this book show you my hope will never really die. My happiness still exists, and my love for you both always will exist.

Sunny Days Ahead

It can be a beautiful day, the sun out shining bright.
It doesnt take long for dark clouds to appear and rain
to overtake the sun.
Sometimes it can seem like all seasons come in a
single day.
But none lasts forever, all come and go.
The sun returns to shine bright again, blue fills the
sky once more.
Like in life the bright days and the dark times all
come and go, some times seem to last forever, some
seem to pass as quickly as they come.

My Story

Life continues on creating my story.
Each day I wake is a chance for a new chapter.
Some days are not so sweet, some pages id be glad to
turn past.
It all comes together in the story the good and the
bad, although life does not always make sense.
Sometimes i wish i could skip ahead afew chapters,
id love to see what the future holds. But in lifes story
there is only now, we must continue on to see the
next chapters, but thats the excitement of reading, and
living. You never know what is to come next. There
are many twists and turns. Many surprises to come.

The sky is crying

Sometimes i dont like the rain, sometimes it makes me sad.
Its like the sky is crying, pouring all its emotions out.
I want to cry with the sky as I look out the window, rain
drops running down fast.
Then i think of all the rain does.
The life it helps, and the life it brings.
I think of the beautiful colours of a rainbow, appearing
thanks to the rain.
I think of the sun after the rain, the happy days to come.
I do like the rain.

Time

Its funny how to sit and watch the clock it seems time
goes so slow. Each minute can feel like forever.
Yet when we are busy time seems to fly by.
The minutes become hours, next thing the day has
gone by.
It depends what way you look at it,
Life can be slow or fast in that moment. But the years
still pass by.

Tamara, My Reason

A reason for living, thats just what i needed. A reason to smile and feel happiness.
Then you came into my life, and gave me just that.
A reason to smile, when im sure i can't.
A reason to laugh at the silliest of things.
A reason to try to be the best version of myself i possibly can.
A reason to pay more attention to the good things in life.
A reason to wake up each day, to live, to love, and I'll always love you.

Lion

Like a lion in the zoo I feel just like you.
You sit in your habitat and stare out, I sit at the window and
stare out into the world.
Watching life pass by. Watching people pass by.
For you they stop and stare. Point, smile and laugh. Some
walk by and not notice you there hiding watching.
Seeing others life go by. Thinking this isn't how life is
meant to be.
Its strange though. Its all you know. It feels so wrong but so
right, perhaps this is not how you imagine it is, but this is
home.
Perhaps this isn't how i imagined life to be, but this is
home.
Remember atleast we are safe and loved both you and I.

Sweet Dreams

It's been a long day i think to myself as i tuck into bed.
I hope i have dreams that are sweet.
I rest my head and begin to count sheep
As i quickly drift off to sleep.
Laying so still, you would never know
In my dreams im off chasing butterflies and watching
puppies play and grow.
In my dreams im just where I love to be, and i love when
you too join me there

Past, Present, Future

I don't let the past defeat me,
It does not define me.
Just like history we cannot deny what happens.
The past may shape me, but it is not me.
Every event comes together to create a story.
My story, your story.
Each is unique, each person, each past.
Every story is destined to be different.
Let history be a lesson, the past cannot be changed.
But dont let it consume you, it is not you.
There may be the past, but there is also the present too.
Following that comes the future, something we should embrace.
We can smile that it is today, the past is gone, the future is yet to come.

Eyes

Sometimes a person's eyes feel Like staring straight
through to someone's soul.
Perhaps I'll forget time and stare for awhile.
Lost in ones blue deep like an ocean.
Fascinated by dark eyes wondering what they hide.
Smiling back at bright eyes that seem to shine like the sun.

Sparkle

Everytime i see a fireplace i think of you, standing proud and tall.
When i hear a dog howl still i remember your sound.
Every spotty dog is beautiful, just none are quite like you.
You left a mark on my heart, without you is a gap i can mever fill.
This special place in my heart will wait for you, i hope some day we can run around over the rainbow forever.
Until then just know i will always love you.

Who Is In The Mirror

I look in the mirror and wonder,
Who is this person i see?
Surely that is not me?
Years have passed by, so fast I can barely recognise the
reflection looking back at me.
As i stare moving closer now i see
The same eyes that always stare back at me.
The same lips form into a smile, my smile.
I look in the mirror and im pleased to see.
I will always be me.

Make Time To Smile

Some days im so busy I don't have time to think. Just trying to get things done it seems it goes from morning to night in a single blink.
Better busy than bored, thats what i say.
But there is too busy, the worst of all.
Being too busy we miss out on things. Lose time for the little things. Small
moments that make memories.
Rushing around we miss that moment extra to smile. Life stops being a joy.
Let's make time for those small things, let's not miss out.
Take time to be happy, find joy in small things, like a beautiful flower, a chirping bird, a smiling child.
There is a whole world filled with beauty.

Don't Quit

I guess i never really lose hope.
I never stop trying even though I always claim to quit.
So many times I say thats it, im done.
Each night I go to bed.
Each morning I wake up to a new day.
Id rather keep continuing to dream about a better day, each day to wake up with a chance of that.
Today is better than yesterday, tomorrow will continue to be better than today.
We just have to keep trying.

Pieces of a Heart

How many pieces can a heart be broken into?
Shattered time and time again, does it become
beyond repair?
No, each piece is taken time and time again. Placed
back together to continue on.
There is always something to love in this world, even
when its just small things found to be loved in life.
There is always a reason to place our hearts back
together and continue on.

A Child's Heart

The way a child can view the world.
With such amazement and joy.
Everything seems exciting and new.
With love and compassion that comes second to none.
They see us all as equal.
Their eyes filled with wonder.
Waiting to see what life has to offer.
How beautiful is a child's heart.

Festival

With bright lights flashing all around
There's so much joy to be found
Rides that go fast or slow
Head up high towards the sky
Or spin around fast feet never touching the ground
Forget your troubles and enjoy life for awhile
With bright lights all around

Life's An Amazing Journey

What the future holds
One never truly knows
From start to finish
Life is a journey
A long path with many choices to be made
A story to be written where you decide each chapter
Life is full of surprises twists and turns
Left yet to discover

Endless stars Endless love

So many stars sparkle in the sky
Light up the dark for you and i
As endless as my love for you
Never truely alone in a world so large
There will always be someone who loves you

Patience

Waiting is hard.
Especially when the wait is long.
The best things take time.
Living takes time.
Being happy can take time too.

A Dad's Poem

When i was little people said some things are black
and white.
This made me think they were speaking of the night.
In the night the stars are white and the sky is black.
I finally figured out what they meant.

Fishers Ghost

There was a man named Fisher
Who hailed from Campbelltown
Until that fateful night
It is said he still frequents the town
Which has now become a city
But he still hangs around
The locals all know him as Fisher's Ghost
The spirit of the man and to him we all raise a toast

CPSIA information can be obtained
at www.ICGtesting.com
Printed in the USA
BVHW050900140623
665885BV00014B/1321

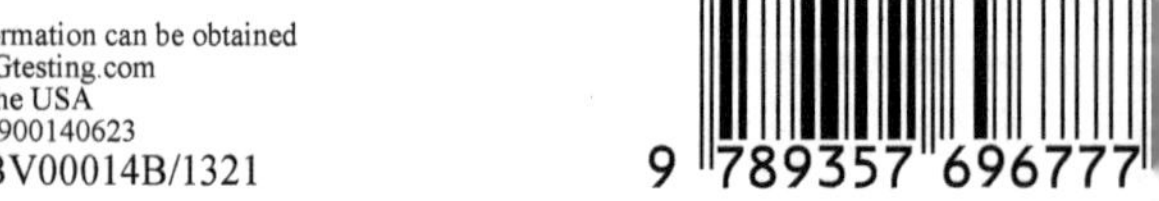